GARDENS
LABYRINTHS
PARADISE

ENRICO RAINERO

photography
Enrico Rainero

editorial collaboration
Giulio Della Santa
Marco Dezzi Bardeschi

graphics
Giorgio Rota

bibliographical research
Stefano Bartalesi,
Carolyn Demcy, Maura Yvonne Duffy,
Ilaria Martin, Brigitte Mauel

iconographical research
Giorgio Rota

color separations
Colorlito, Milano

printing
Elcograf, Beverate (Como)

editorial direction
© 1985 studio Enrico Rainero, Florence

translation
Patricia Schultz

ISBN 88-85700-06-3

The owners of all gardens photographed are
gratefully acknowledged for their
collaboration in the realization of this book.

INTRODUCTION

This book offers an itinerary of invention and fantasy within the ideal garden, created by joining together naturalistic and artistic phenomena, and the mythological and allegorical wonders of the centuries-old history of man and his garden.

The three chapters of this book will be the imaginary foot paths that will guide the visitor through the history of man's relationship with nature.

The first chapter sees the birth of "vegetation" as the allegory of the birth of life; the elements – water, air, fire, earth – are united in a primitive nature that was then utilized by man for his own survival. Intervention begins, together with a gradual transformation of the terrain and landscape.

The second chapter begins with the interpretation and use of nature as pleasure or as an esthetic motive. From the Medieval "hortus conclusus" to the majestic gardens of the Medici Villas, these historical gardens increasingly gained an architectural significance. They specialized in a growing, symbolic value at once esthetic, political, mystical.

Exceptional allegorical representations triumph in the third chapter: man's initial disorientation in science, knowledge and the spirit are represented by the "dark forest" and the Labyrinth whose recurrence of paths scatter and confuse human attempts to achieve...? Each effort is expressed in ways that are recreational or spiritual, mystical or satanic; man's internal search for Paradise is represented by the secret garden while the garden theatre repeats a performance to infinity.

The theme is developed along two parallel journeys: the first by images, the second by a wealth of quotations that emphasize the photographs.

We have played with the subjects photographed, interpreting them graphically and accentuating the structure that was at times symbolic, at times esthetic; we have given them the rhythm of the seasons' cycles.

Finding ourselves each time more involved in this journey, we realized the validity of the warning "One does not build labyrinths without getting lost."

Enrico Rainero

INDEX

G E N E S I S

Land, Water, Air, together mixed and blent; –
Land stable to no foot, – Water which gave
No space to swim, – and Air devoid of light.
No proper form to aught: – perpetual jar
And conflict, through the mass, of Hot to Cold
Opposed, of Wet to Dry, of Soft to Hard,
Of Light to Heavy, – till the Power divine
And kindlier Nature bade their contest cease,
Dividing Earth from Heaven, and Sea from Earth,
And liquid Æther from our grosser Air:
Which, from the blind heap where they lay, evolved,
And each to separate place assigned, she linked
Thenceforward in the holy bond of Peace.

OVID

Ere Earth and Ocean and all-covering Heaven Grew into separate form,
great Nature's face
Through all existence but one aspect wore: –
Chaos 'twas called; – a rude unfeatured mass, –
A mere vast weight inert, – discordant seeds
Of ill-matched things in one huge heap compressed.

OVID

△ Hot water spring at Saturnia   Ferrous slag from work at the mines of Colline Metallifere ▷

For Winter came: the wind was his whip:
One choppy finger was on his lip:
He had torn the cataracts from the hills
And they clanked at his girdle like manacles;

His breath was a chain which without a sound
The earth, and the air, and the water bound;
He came, fiercely driven, in his chariot-throne
By the tenfold blasts of the Arctic zone.

PERCY BYSSHE SHELLEY

Chestnut forest at Marradi △

△ *Forests and pastures in the Gran Sasso*

Spontaneous Earth, unwounded by the stroke
Of share or harrow, gave them all her store.
Content with food unlabored, fruit they plucked
Of arbutus, or mountain-strawberry,
Cornels, black berries from the thorny bush,
And acorns dropped from Jove's wide-branching tree.
Amidst eternal Spring, the gentle breath
Of Zephyr fostering cheered the unsown flowers.
Earth gave her corn unploughed, and, year by year,
Unfallowed, whitened fresh with plenteous grain.
With flood of milk and nectar ran the streams,
And from the oak the honeyed gold distilled.

OVID

Mediterranean vegetation on the beach of the Parco dell'Uccellina ▷   *Meadow of poppies and umbrella pines* ▷

While yet the spring is young, while earth unbinds
Her frozen bosom to the western winds;
While mountain snows dissolve against the sun,
And streams yet new, from precipices run;
E'en in this early dawning of the year,
Produce the plough, and yoke the sturdy steer,
And goad him till he groans beneath his toil,
Till the bright share is buried in the soil.
That crop rewards the greedy peasant's pains,
Which twice the sun, and twice the cold sustains,
And bursts the crowded barns with more than promised gains.
But, ere we stir the yet unbroken ground,
The various course of seasons must be found;
The weather, and the setting of the winds,
The culture suiting to the several kinds
Of seeds and plants, and what will thrive and rise,
And what the genius of the soil denies.
This ground with Bacchus, that with Ceres, suits:
That other loads the trees with happy fruits:
A fourth, with grass unbidden, decks the ground.

VIRGIL

△ Plowing

Wheat field. In the background, cypresses mark the property's border ▷

(...)
What mysterious thought
moves the wheat?
What rhythm of dreamy sadness
stirs the crops?

The wheat seems like tired birds
that can no longer fly!
They have small heads
with a brain of pure gold
and have a peaceful expression.

They all think about the same thing,
they all have
a profound secret to meditate.
They snatch from the earth its living gold
and, like the sun's sweet bees, drink
the warm rays they wear
to form the flour's soul.

Oh what happy sadness you give me,
delicious wheat!
You come from the most profound age,
singing in the Bible
and giving, when the silence withers you,
a concert of lyres.

You abound to nourish man.
But look at the white daisies
and the lilies that are born, yes!
Golden mummies in the fields!
The wild flower is born for dreams
and you for life!

FEDERICO GARCIA LORCA

But when the grain is ripe it should be quickly harvested before it can be parched by the heat of the summer sun, which is most severe at the rising of the Dog-star; (...) for which reason there should be no delay, but when the crop is even golden yellow, before the grains have entirely hardened and after they have taken on a reddish color, the harvest should be gathered, so that the grain may grow larger on the floor and in the stack rather than in the field.

LUCIUS JUNIUS MODERATUS COLUMELLA

◁ *The hills of Volterra*   *Sienese countryside after the threshing in June* △

As legions in the field their front display,
To try the fortune of some doubtful day,
And move to meet their foes with sober pace,
Strict to their figure, though in wider space,
Before the battle joins, while from afar
The field yet glitters with the pomp of war,
And equal Mars, like an impartial lord,
Leaves all to fortune, and the dint of sword:
So let thy vines in intervals be set,
But not their rural discipline forget;
Indulge their width, and add a roomy space,
That their extremest lines may scarce embrace:
Nor this alone to indulge a vain delight,
And make a pleasing prospect for the sight,
But for the ground itself; this only way
Can equal vigour to the plants convey,
Which, crowded, want the room, their branches to
display.

VIRGIL

Vineyards of the Chianti hills ▷

Architecture of Chianti landscape △

*There are two seasons for pruning; but the better time is in the spring, before the
shoot puts forth its buds. (...)
To us it seems that plants should not be held back by close pruning unless they are
very weak, in the first year that they are set out they should be aided, every month
while they are in leaf, by frequent digging and by leaf-pruning, so that they may
gain strength and support not more than one branch of firm wood. In the autumn,
or in the spring if it is more convenient, they should be freed from secondary shoots
which the leaf-pruner had left on the upper part; and so they should be placed upon
the frame.*

LUCIUS JUNIUS MODERATUS COLUMELLA

△ *Centuries-old olive trees after pruning time at S. Antimo*

So that, unless the land with daily care
Is exercised, and, with an iron war
Of rakes and harrows, the proud foes expelled,
And birds with clamours frighted from the field –
Unless the boughs are lopped that shade the plain,
And heaven invoked with vows for fruitful rain –
On others' crops you may with envy look,
And shake for food the long-abandoned oak.

VIRGIL

Hill and neglected olive grove in the Maremma △

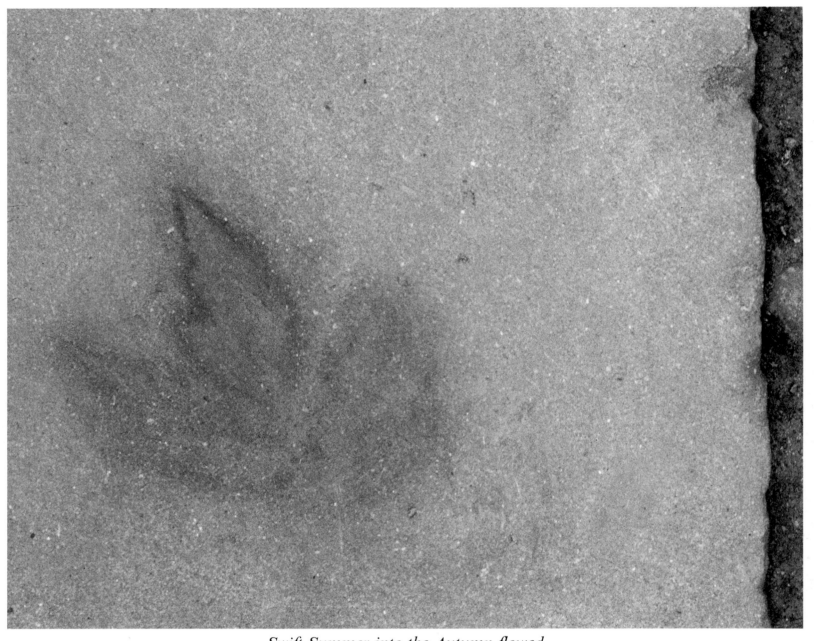

Swift Summer into the Autumn flowed,
And frost in the mist of the morning rode,
Though the noonday sun looked clear and bright,
Mocking the spoil of the secret night.

The rose-leaves, like flakes of crimson snow,
Paved the turf and the moss below.
The lilies were drooping, and white, and wan,
Like the head and the skin of a dying man.

PERCY BYSSHE SHELLEY

△ *Imprint of a leaf on pietraserena after a storm*

THE HISTORICAL GARDEN

We must not forget cheerful gardens full of marvelous plants; with an arcade from which one can enjoy the sun or shade. There should also be an "open space" from which small brooks branch out in several directions.
The positioning of the plants – the evergreens – will determine the pathways.
On a sheltered side one should plant a box hedge; which, in fact, would suffer and wither if exposed to direct light or the elements.
Myrtle is to be planted in sunny areas because it is said that summer heat is good for it. (...) Nor can ivy-covered cypresses be ignored. They can form circles, semicircles and other geometric designs to be used near the buildings bordered by a series of laurel, cedar, juniper and climbing plants which will braid and interwine among them.
Fiteone d'Agrigento had 300 stone vases in his home, each equal to 100 amphorae. Such vases go best in front of fountains, in ornamental gardens.
Just as in ancient times vines were attached to the tops of marble columns in such a way as to grow across, one to the other, thus covering the paths in the garden.
Rows of trees should be spaced at an equal distance from each other with opposite 'corners' forming what is called the "quincunx".
The garden will stay green by planting rare types of grasses or those herbs used for medicinal purposes. I like the old custom where farmers honored their lords by forming their names in a section of the garden using box hedges or sweet smelling plants. Hedges intertwined with roses, hazel or pomegranate.
A poet once said, "Bushes yield cornels and plums; oaks and ilex (holm-oaks) provide a lot of food for the cattle and plenty of shade for the owner".
This solution, however, is more suitable on land full of fruit trees than in a garden. We don't agree with the saying which tradition attributes to Democritus: "He who surrounds his Garden with rocks or a stone wall is not wise." In fact one must protect himself against vandals, anyway!
We will not reprove the placing of silly statues in gardens as long as there is nothing obscene. These should be the characteristics of a garden!

LEON BATTISTA ALBERTI

Barco Reale at the Medici Villa of Artimino ▷　　　*Grape vine ▷*　　　*Walls of the city of Artimino ▷*

36

I chanced an old Corycian swain to know,
Lord of few acres, and those barren too,
Unfit for sheep or vines, and more unfit to sow;
Yet labouring well his little spot of ground,
Some scattering pot-herbs here and there he found,
Which cultivated with his daily care,
And bruised with vervain, were his frugal fare.
And, calling western winds, accused the spring of sloth.

VIRGIL

◁ *Farmhouse courtyards*

Manfredi Garden △

41

Capponi Garden △   *Wooden steps in the Horti Leonini* ▷   *Secret garden of the Villa La Pietra* ▷

Medici Villa at Artimino △

△ *Medici Villa at Petraia*

Garden and countryside of Castello di Brolio ▷

And from this undefilèd Paradise
The flowers (as an infant's awakening eyes
Smile on its mother, whose singing sweet
Can first lull, and at last must awaken it),

When Heaven's blithe winds had unfolded them,
As mine-lamps enkindle a hidden gem,
Shone smiling to Heaven, and every one
Shared joy in the light of the gentle sun.

PERCY BYSSHE SHELLEY

◁ *Medici Garden at Petraia* △   *Palagio Garden* ▷   *Medici Garden at Petraia* ▷

△ *Santini Torrigiani Garden at Camigliano* ▷   *Medici Garden at Petraia* ▷   *Winter at Poggio a Caiano* ▷

There were roses snow white and brilliant red:
the sunshine unfolded one, petal by petal;
tight at first, then opened and ruffled;
another younger one came loose
at the bud; there were still others
whose closed petals refused the air;
another, falling, bloomed on the ground.

And so I saw them born and dying,
living their beauty in less than an hour.
When, languid and pale, I saw them
fall to earth, it came to me
what a vain thing is the youthful blossom.
Each tree has its flower, then immediately
the leaves unfold in the sun
when they feel the air.
Small fruits still unformed hold on,
at times slowly growing to such a size
that the strong boughs dangerously bend
from their weight; soon they grow used to
the increase and they now manage.

Autumn arrives and the ripe, sweet apples
are gathered and, this beautiful weather gone,
flowers, fruits and leaves are shed.
Pick the rose, oh nymph, now is the time.

LORENZO IL MAGNIFICO

Greenhouse of Poggio a Caiano ▷ Allegories on the frontispiece of the Medici Villa of Poggio a Caiano ▷ The four seasons ▷

◁ *Gamberaia Garden*

◁ *Garden of la Pietra* △   *Statue in the Garden of la Pietra* ▷   *Statue in the Torrigiani Garden in Florence* ▷

A Sensitive Plant in a garden grew,
And the young winds fed it with silver dew,
And it opened its fan-like leaves to the light,
And closed them beneath the kisses of Night.

And the Spring arose on the garden fair,
Like the Spirit of Love felt everywhere;
And each flower and herb on Earth's dark breast
Rose from the dreams of its wintry rest.

The snowdrop, and then the violet,
Arose from the ground with warm rain wet,
And their breath was mixed with fresh odour, sent
From the turf, like the voice and the instrument.

And the rose like a nymph to the bath addressed,
Which unveiled the depth of her glowing breast,
Till, fold after fold, to the fainting air
The soul of her beauty and love lay bare:

And the wand-like lily, which lifted up,
As a Maenad, its moonlight-coloured cup,
Till the fiery star, which is its eye.
Gazed through clear dew on the tender sky;

And the jessamine faint, and the sweet tuberose,
The sweetest flower for scent that blows;
And all rare blossoms from every clime
Grew in that garden in perfect prime.

PERCY BYSSHE SHELLEY

△ *Beds at Garzoni, fine example of topiary art*

Garzoni Garden ▷

Above the soaring arches, which looked as though they supported the very dome of Heaven, gardens extended which were so spacious and magnificent that even at ground-level they would be hard to lay out. Through the luminous crenellations could be seen the verdure of the fragrant trees, which were a delight in the summer, and in winter remained a mass of blossom and ripe fruit. / Trees as noble do not grow outside these lovely gardens, nor do such roses, violets and lilies, amarants and jasmine. You will observe, anywhere else, how all in one day a flower will be born, live out its term and die, drooping its head on its bereaved stalk, for it is subject to the changing seasons. / Here, though, everything remained verdant green; the flowers bloomed in perpetual radiance, not through any beneficent working of Nature.

LUDOVICO ARIOSTO

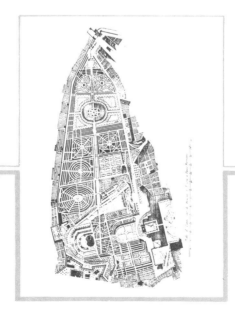

△ *The flight of steps that leads to the statue of Fame in the Garzoni Garden.*

Statue of Daphne in the Garzoni Garden ▷

△ *Medici Garden at Careggi*　　　　*Dwarf in the Medici Garden at Careggi, allegory of political power* ▷　　　　*The Horti Leonini* ▷

In the middle of this garden, what seemed more delightful than any thing else, was a plot of ground like a meadow; the grass of a deep green, spangled with a thousand different flowers, and set round with orange and cedar trees, whose branches were stored with ripe fruit and blossoms, at the same time affording a most pleasing object to the eye, as well as a grateful odor to the smell.
In the centre of this meadow was a fountain of white marble, beautifully carved; and (whether by a natural or artificial spring, I know not) from a figure standing on a column in the midst of the fountain, a jet of water spouted up, which made a most agreeable sound in its fall: the water which came from thence ran through the meadow by a secret passage.

GIOVANNI BOCCACCIO

Medici Garden of Castello ▷

Medici Garden of Castello △

△ *Statues of ancient patrician Romans in the Medici Garden of Castello*

△ *Medici Garden of Castello*

Statue representing Winter ▷

△ *Green tunnel in the Boboli Garden*

Satyr in the basin of the Boboli Garden ▷

△ *Detail of islet in the Boboli Garden* ▷

Islet in the Boboli Garden ▷

104

Coldly, sadly descends
The autumn evening. The field
Strewn with its dark yellow drifts
Of wither'd leaves, and the elms,
Fade into dimness apace,
Silent.

MATTHEW ARNOLD

△ *The large fountain in form of amphitheatre of the Villa Reale at Marlia*

Details of the fountain ▷

She sprinkled bright water from the stream
On those that were faint with the sunny beam;
And out of the cups of the heavy flowers
She emptied the rain of the thunder-showers.
She lifted their heads with her tender hands,
And sustained them with rods and osier-bands;
If the flowers had been her own infants, she
Could never have nursed them more tenderly.

PERCY BYSSHE SHELLEY

Statue representing the Arno River at the Villa Reale at Marlia ▷

THE GARDEN
OF DESIRE

Now to th'ascent of that steep savage Hill
Satan had journied on, pensive and slow;
But further way found none, so thick entwin'd,
As one continu'd brake, the undergrowth
Of shrubs and tangling bushes had perplext
All path of Man or Beast that past that way:
One Gate there onely was, and that look'd East
On th' other side: which when th' arch-fellon saw
Due entrance he disdaind, and in contempt,
At one slight bound high overleap'd all bound
Of Hill or highest Wall, and sheer within
Lights on his feet.

JOHN MILTON

Forest in the winter fog ▷

It is not God's will that what he created for man's benefit should remain hidden. And even if certain things are hidden, He has not left anything without external clues, visible by means of special signs: similar to the man who, unearthing a buried treasure, marks the spot so that he may return.

PARACELSO

Pinocchio Garden at Collodi ▷

The Turtle in the Park of Bomarzo ▷

△ *Dragon in the Park of Bomarzo.*

An ancient Roman Legionary is overpowered by Hannibal's elephant ▷

*Nor can we allow anybody to say that in some of these palaces in the Indies, in the meadows around them, grow from the earth some lumps of natural stone in which they have sculptured their idols and some figures shaped as their strange animals.
If there were in our parts of the country stones like those, they could become beautiful sculptures: statues, colossi or other amusing inventions; as at Bomarzo where we can see these natural stones quarried, made of more than one big block, representing a mask, whose mouth serves for a door and whose windows are the eyes and whose tongue, inside, serves for a table and teeth for seats. And when, inside, the table is prepared and lit by lamps among the dishes, from far off, appears a terrifying mask.*

G.V. SODERINI

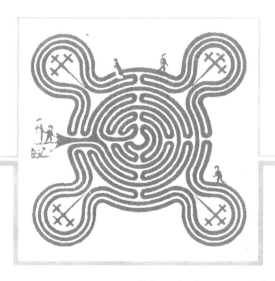

"All thought flies away." Orco's gigantic mouth, gateway to Hell ▷

The palace is called Pratolino; seen from a distance the building is nothing exceptional but from close up it is truly beautiful, although not like the best in France. They say there are one hundred twenty furnished rooms; we saw ten or twelve of the best: the furniture is pleasant but not magnificent. What is really extraordinary is a grotto with many niches and divisions and it far surpasses anything we have ever seen anywhere; it is encrusted and covered everywhere by a material that they say is dug out of certain mountains and then held into place here by invisible screws. Not only does the action of the water create music and harmory, but it puts into motion numerous statues and doors resulting in various movements such as animals that dive to drink and other such things. By means of a unique mechanism, the grotto fills up with water, the seats spray water on you up to the thighs and, if fleeing from the grotto, you try to climb the steps to the castle, every other step sprays you – for whomever would like a similar amusement – a thousand jets douse you until you arrive at the top.

The beauty and magnificence of this place cannot be described in detail. Above the palace there exists an avenue 500 steps long; on both sides every five or ten steps, there are long and beautiful props in sculpted stone, and next to these props appear small fountains spraying from the wall in such a way that there does not exist a single point along the entire avenue lacking in water spouts. At the end you can see a beautiful fountain flowing into a grand basin by means of a marble statue of a women intent upon doing her wash. She is wringing out a sheet of white marble that drips with water while underneath a tub holds water that seems to boil. In the palace there is a table, also of marble, with six seats, at which each guest can lift by means of a ring, a piece of the tabletop and underneath – still in the table itself – there is a hollowed out area; in each cavity there rushes a jet of water that keeps cool the glass of each guest; in the center there is a larger one for a bottle. We also saw vast pits in the earth to save large quantities of snow all year round, left upon a bed of hay; it is then covered with another layer of hay in the form of a pyramid, similar to a small hut. There are an infinity of reservoirs; the body of a giant has been built whose eye is three forearms wide with the rest in proportion, from which springs an abundant stream. Reservoirs and basins are everywhere and all of this comes from a few underground springs.

MICHEL DE MONTAIGNE

In the walls adorned with sponges are two small houses or workshops. One is the forge of Vulcan in which many different figurines work as ironsmiths with anvils, hammers, iron tools and everything necessary for their art. Not far away is the other building, a mill, where many different figures carry a sack on their shoulder or are involved in other jobs about the mill, including the task of putting the mill stone into action which, thanks to the water power, turns.

Far off, one notices a hunt with many animals quickly being chased after by hunters. Nearby, other animals can be seen, including two ducks that lower their heads to drink. But before this, there are some marvelous 'water tricks', among which is a serpent who turns, various animals and different kinds of trees that are filled with many birds who sing in turn.

Above the door, or gate, through which the shepherdess passes, there is an owl that moves towards the birds as well as two other beautiful and stupendous things that would take too much to describe in detail, all of which operate by different machinations triggered by water. The dome and walls of these grottos are adorned with various divisions of stones of many color, shells, mother of pearl, and so many other truly remarklable things. And so, many are the mysterious devices and bazaar inventions that shower the visitor with water. Those that attract the most curious looker-on, cannot be escaped from and it seems almost impossible that the human mind, while capable of imagining them, could ever produce them.

One moves on to find the beautiful and magnificent staircase under which are two gracefully ornate grottos. In the first one there are two small ponds, one on top of the other, in which some men with sticks are killing frogs. In the other small grotto, also skillfully ornate, a small animal called a weasel runs behind a snake.

Inside both of these small grottos can be found two stools that invite the visitor to sit and observe better these bazaar inventions; but upon sitting, one is showered with water that falls from some openings above.

Owed to the talent of the hydraulic experts, many other tricks as well douse the outsider with water.

Along the sides of these grottos there are two very ornate iron gates, one to the east and the other to the west. Beyond these, another large gate has been placed to the south; one must pass through here to reach the above described grotto of the deluge.

SGRILLI

Lucifer in the Grotto of Gamberaia ▷

△ *Grotto of Neptune with "water tricks" in the Garzoni Garden*

The birth of animals, allegory in the Grotto of Castello ▷

There is a cave, all overgrown with trailing odorous plants,
Which curtain out the day with leaves and flowers,
And paved with veinèd emerald, and a fountain
Leaps in the midst with an awakening sound.
From its curved roof the mountain's frozen tears
Like snow, or silver, or long diamond spires,
Hang downward, raining forth a doubtful light:
And there is heard the ever-moving air,
Whispering without from tree to tree, and birds,
And bees; and all around are mossy seats,
And the rough walls are clothed with long soft grass;
A simple dwelling, which shall be our own;

We will entangle buds and flowers and beams
Which twinkle on the fountain's brim, and make
Strange combinations out of common things,
Like human babes in their brief innocence.

The wandering voices and the shadows these
Of all that man becomes, the mediators
Of that best worship love, by him and us
Given and returned; swift shapes and sounds, which grow
More fair and soft as man grows wise and kind,
And, veil by veil, evil and error fall:
Such virtue has the cave and place around.

PERCY BYSSHE SHELLEY

<Frontispiece of the Boboli Grotto*   *Helen and Paris in the Boboli Grotto* ▷

Of Eden, where delicious Paradise,
Now nearer, Crowns with her enclosure green,
As with a rural mound the champain head
Of a steep wilderness, whose hairie sides
With thicket overgrown, grottesque and wilde,
Access deni'd; and over head up grew
Insuperable highth of loftiest shade,
Cedar, and Pine, and Firr, and branching Palm,
A Silvan Scene, and as the ranks ascend
Shade above shade, a woodie Theatre
Of stateliest view. Yet higher then thir tops
The verdurous wall of Paradise up sprung.

JOHN MILTON

△ *Cypresses in the Sienese countryside*

*Therefore the Lord God sent him forth from the garden of Eden, to till the ground
from which he was taken.
He drove out the man; and at the east of the garden of Eden he placed the
cherubim, and a flaming sword which turned every way, to guard the way to the tree
of life.*

GENESIS

◁ *Wall encircling the Certosa of Calci*   ◁ *Fresco in the cloister of the Abbey of Monteoliveto Maggiore*   *Abbey of S. Antimo △*

"In summer or spring, through the variety of its plants, each then adorned with its flowers, this garden sings better the praises of the Creator," Severinus said, somewhat apologetically. "But even now, in winter, the herbalist's eye sees through the dry branches the plants that will come, and he can tell you that this garden is richer than any herbal ever was, and more varicolored, beautiful as the illuminations are in those volumes. Furthermore, good herbs grow also in winter, and I preserve others gathered and ready in the pots in my laboratory... there are no plants good for food that are not good for treating the body, too, provided they are taken in the right quantity. Only excess makes them cause illness."

UMBERTO ECO

Small country church in Radicondoli ▷

Chapels in the Forest of S. Vivaldo ▷

Hide from me things far away,
thou pale and impalpable fog,
thou vapor, that still mountest upward
at dawn,
from crashings at night, and from quivering
vibrations in air!

Hide from me things far away,
oh, hide from me that which is dead!
The hedge let me see of the orchard,
that only,
the wall that has crevices flowering
with valerian bloom.

Hide from me things far away:
the things are all drunken with tears!
Two trees let me see, peach and apple,
just these,
that give me their honeys delicious
for my crust of bread.

Hide from me things far away,
that will me to love and to rove!
That white let me see of the roadway
there, only,
which one day by me must be traversed
to slow tolling bells.

Hide from me things far away,
hide swift from the flight of my heart!
The cypress tree let me see, only,
afar,
and here but this orchard, beside which
my dog lies, asleep.

GIOVANNI PASCOLI

◁ *Shrine in the Sesto Fiorentino countryside*

△ *Hermitage at Camaldoli* ▷

In this pleasant soile
His farr more pleasant Garden God ordaind;
Out of the fertil ground he caus'd to grow
All trees of noblest kind for sight, smell, taste;
And all amid them stood the Tree of Life,
High eminent, blooming Ambrosial Fruit
Of vegetable Gold; and next to Life
Our Death the Tree of Knowledge grew fast by,
Knowledge of Good bought dear by knowing ill.
Southward through Eden went a River large,
Nor chang'd his course, but through the shaggie hill
Pass'd underneath ingulft, for God had thrown
That Mountain as his Garden mould high rais'd
Upon the rapid current, which through veins
Of porous Earth with kindly thirst up drawn,
Rose a fresh Fountain, and with many a rill
Waterd the Garden.

JOHN MILTON

Cloister of S. Francesco di Fiesole ▷

Cloister of the Certosa di Calci

Without moving any part of my body, I look for every part of the Ocean, and encircle all this round ball, which is called earth.
I try to see how many seas cover it, and how many lakes and rivers flow through it, how many islands, ports, rocks, mountains, plains, castles, towns, provinces and regions there are. And going into it, I try to see veins of gold, silver and other metals, together in the center of the earth. And being dissatisfied with these base things, my thought and my mind fly, running from one sphere to another... I finally penetrate as far as Him... God. And then absolutely astonished I begin methodically to consider again things made by Him and by this way, rising and sinking, I have perfect cognisance of this world.

B. TAEGIO

Inside of the Basilica of S. Galgano ▷

A garden locked is my sister, my bride,
a garden locked, a fountain sealed.
Your shoots are an orchard of pomegranates
with all choicest fruits,
henna with nard,
nard and saffron, calamus and cinnamon,
with all trees of frankincense,
myrrh and aloes,
with all chief spices-
a garden fountain,
a well of living water and
flowing streams from Lebanon.
Awake, O north wind,
and come, O south wind!
Blow upon my garden,
let its fragrance be wafted abroad.

SONG OF SOLOMON

△ *Secret garden in Lucca*

Secret garden in Lucca △

△ *Della Gherardesca Garden*

Entrance to the Garden I Tatti ▷

That garden sweet, that lady fair,
And all sweet shapes and odours there,
In truth have never passed away:
'Tis we, 'tis ours, are changed; not they.

For love, and beauty, and delight,
There is no death nor change: their might
Exceeds our organs, which endure
No light, being themselves obscure.

PERCY BYSSHE SHELLEY

Santini Torrigiani Garden in Camigliano ▷

My beloved had a vineyard on a very fertile hill.
He digged it and cleared it of stones, and planted it with choice vines; he built a
watchtower in the midst of it, and hewed out a wine vat in it; and he looked for it to
yield grapes, but it yielded wild grapes.
I will remove its hedge, and it shall be devoured;
I will break down its wall, and it shall be trampled down.
I will make it a waste; it shall not be pruned or hoed, and briers and thorns
shall grow up.

ISAIAH

◁ *"Secret and quiet place to breathe" in the Manfredi Garden*   △ *Tiepidarium Roster at the Horticulture Garden* ▷

We are therefore bound to the Engine of all by three ropes, to intelligence by the Intelligence, to the "idols" by the "Idol", to nature by Nature, as, in the womb, the fetus is bound to the whole body of the mother by uninterrupted cords.

MARSILIO FICINO

△ *Olive trees grow atop Lucca's Torre Guinigi*

△ Sculpture displayed in the Horti Leorini

The whole Pitti theatre was full of star-shaped lights, hanging at a proportioned height from some bitumen frames which for this effect were created in a masterly manner. These lamps were more than sufficient to overcome the darkness of the night and nevertheless in order to enact in the best way the brightness of the day in the most dense obscurity; some other lamps in the same shape were arranged under the lowest balustrades around the theatre; they were hanging from some iron arms, not very distant one from another, and were blazing brightly because the tin-covered wall reflected back the light of the lamps (on the Pitti side).

It appeared to be a sylvan scene which re-enacted the woody nature, as I said before, so well one could not distinguish the real from the false.

FERDINANDO ROSSI

Theatre of la Pietra ▷

Boboli Amphitheatre ▷

Veglio is called in their language Aloodyn (Alaodin).
In a valley, between two mountains, he had the biggest most beautiful garden in the world created; there he had all kinds of fruit and the most beautiful of palaces in the world, all painted in gold colors with birds and animals. There were conduits there: one for water, one for honey and one for wine. There were pages and damsels, the most beautiful in the world, who could sing, play and dance in a wonderful way; and Veglio let them believe that it was Paradise.

MARCO POLO

HISTORICAL NOTES

poggio a caiano

The colonnade of the Villa at Poggio was often used as the scenic backdrop for theatrical productions. Architectural design thereafter became a place of performance bound by a double link to the surrounding nature. The garden contained a labyrinth of disorientation, fountain-like 'games' of purified water and a Botanical Garden that taught the wise ways of plant life while a zoological garden dealt with the animal world; the allegories on the frontispiece of the villa represented the unchangeable astrological laws necessary for stellar harmony.
From cosmogony descended the solution to the problem of knowledge.
Parterres (division of planes) are made up of geometric shapes that symbolized the plan of the universe.
The frieze's first panel represents cosmogony. In the center is the progenitor goddess from whom are born winged figures; the snake that bites its own neck symbolizes the course and recurrence of history. Other characters recall the eternal rules that guide the world, generated by the gods.
In the second panel is the dance of the Corybants (priests of the goddess Cibele who solemnized the feastdays). The nanny-goat Amaltea suckles Jove and the beehives supply the honey representing the artist's wish for an abundant life.
In the third panel, Giano Bifronte controls the passage of time in the months of the year.
In the fourth panel, the rhythm of rural labor determines the passing of the seasons.
In the fifth panel, the allegories of Ovid's "Metamorphosis" depict the life of day and night.

theatre-garden

The theatre-garden was the ultimate expression of the allegory of life and a place where it was possible to represent everything, thanks to comedy, its masks and its shams. The theatre triumphantly entered to take part in the garden.
Already, the natural tendency to use the green space around the villa first as a meeting place, then for celebrations, parties and public demonstrations had introduced the use of outdoor productions; but the culmination of the reversal of roles was when the spectator himself, moving within the space of the garden, became the protagonist of the performance.
All of the surrounding choreography was a metaphor of a repeated scene in the time and space of the infinite. Masks, like the statues and supporting casts, represented man, the intermingling of roles and the fraud of his life. The mask became the emblem of the 16th century, result of the necessity to "represent" that which was no longer truth, certainty, dogma, infallibility.
By creating the theatre-garden, man reached the summit of his intellectual manipulation of nature.

labyrinth

The labyrinth was a philosophical representation of the search for new paths of knowledge which were imprisoned, however, in the mental snares of centuries-old traditions. The labyrinth mapped out the roads of life, bristling from digressions and returns. This artful Renaissance garden, supreme synthesis of symbolization, was built with low hedges for a simple, esthetic design; its extreme and exceptionally sophisticated elaboration of "topiary art" was typical of the Italian garden. Labyrinths were also built with high hedge barriers whose purpose was the amusement of those who would actually lose their way or with a maze that was not physically obligatory but rather a capricious passage with returns and paths of allegorical and psychological significance, such as at Bomarzo.

grottos

Symbolism and reality, art and nature come together in the theme of the grotto. Shadow and light, deception and truth, simplicity and bravado. The grotto represents the gateway to the underground afterworld, entrance to immortality. One returns to magic and the occult.
Ovid, in "Metamorphosis", saw animals born from the sands of the Nile; Tribolo sculpted that very moment of magic in the grotto of Castello (1560) when the unicorn excelled above all other animals, symbol of the Sovereign Prince.
The concept of shapeless matter that takes the form of the human body is emphasized in the grotto of Buontalenti at Boboli (1583). The frescos on the walls augment ambiguity by playing with the fake stalactites, creating an effect of allusion and reality and two and three dimensional scenery.
Light filters through an acquarium at the top of the grotto. Fish in continuous motion create a perpetually changing play of shadow and light. The figures of Paris and Helen continue their timeless love story; their group of sculptures is set in a second grotto, after the grotto depicting the birth of life from gray matter (with Michelangelo's statues "The Slaves") and before the grotto of Venus, symbol of perfect beauty, eternal love and the divine origin of life.

garden of the castle

The expansion of Medici power (1540) found a maximum need for expression under Cosimo I. Patronage and magnificence mirrored the princely power: antique statues of the classical divinities found throughout the garden were silent witnesses to it, authorities by virtue of their bond with history and harmonious insertion in nature.

The order formed by the garden's geometry did not conflict with the chaos of the labyrinth (today destroyed). Order was, in fact, the solution to the search for the right path of the labyrinth.

The hydrographic system came down from the higher grounds of the garden, like the rivers that flow down from the mountains (the Appennines) and extend across the plain; such was the power of the Prince over the villa's garden and his political territories. Behind water, the fluid of life, was God, Lord of the Universe; above water, life of the garden, was the Prince, Lord of Florence.

CERTOSA DI CALCI (Pisa)

The monastery was founded in 1366.

The monks' cells, nucleus for their autonomous life, faced the Large Cloister which was surrounded by a columned arcade. Each monk had two small rooms for work and prayer and a small garden to cultivate. In the center of the Cloister there stands a stately fountain from 1640; to one side, a small area was used as a cementery for priests.

Communal life revolved around the Refectory and in the church which was later restored in the 17th century. Each monk had a small chapel at his disposal in which to celebrate daily mass.

Lay brothers were used for many services, particularly the farming of the surrounding land enclosed by a high wall, since the monks of noble blood were not expected to dedicate themselves to such activities.

Currently, the Certosa is uninhabited but it is possible to visit with a guide.

HERMITAGE OF CAMALDOLI (Arezzo)

Immersed in a large forest, this hermitage was built about 1012-1024.

Saint Romualdo was given the land by the Bishop of Arezzo; then called "Campo Malduli" and situated on the Appennino Tosco Emilio mountain range, the land was given for the use of the hermit monks who followed the rules laid down by Saint Benedict.

On this site Romualdo built the Church dedicated to the Transfiguration and five cells to house the first hermits. This hermitage is typical in that the cells were built like small houses, each one separate from the next. Each house was made up of the following: a studio with a table, a bed whose mattress was a large sack stuffed with hay or leaves, a small library, a niche to store wood, a room with a fountain from which the hermits drew water and a small garden.

Some years later Romualdo began the construction of Fontebuono in an area closer to the valley in order to welcome travellers and pilgrims. After a few years both the hermitage and the new building were enlarged so that the latter became the actual monastery for monks and lay brothers.

The hermits and monks were practical connoisseurs of medicinal plants, preparing infusions and balms for the monastery's pharmacy which is still open today.

GARDEN PARK OF BOMARZO (Viterbo)

The Garden of Bomarzo was created in 1552 by the wish and inspiration of Prince Pier Francesco Orsini. The architect Pirro Ligorio created what is still considered today a truly singular work. We find ourselves at the entrance to a park that is almost unreal and fantastic, where mythology and allegory seem to express a symbolic thought, as if the world of the dead was united to the forces of nature. Many statues, in fact, support such a concept: Mars, Hercules, Ceres, Proserpine.

The definition given Bomarzo is *"Something that resembles only itself"* implying that the influence of the landscape is so peculiar that it is called the "Sacred Wood". Entering, one immediately finds the inscriptions of Orsini

himself, meant to help the visitor better understand the oddity of the park. But mystery is in the air, stimulating new and contradictory sensations.

The wood is situated on a terrain rich with ravines and gorges and enormous rocks sculpted in singular, mythical themes. Spontaneous vegetation creates a unique atmosphere around these "monsters". Such a sensation also comes from the magnificence and size of these statues; for example, the group that represents "the fight between the giants" in which Hercules and Cancus express the struggle between good and bad. The expression given Hercules is serene despite the cruel action. Of unique beauty is the group of sculpture represented by the "turtle, woman, whale" in which the woman standing on a globe represents winged victory. Further on we find a theatre which, according to the ancient Romans, was to have been a part of every garden.

The enormous head of a man with a threatening expression is a disconcerting sight; better known as "Orco", his mouth is said to be the entranceway to Hell. The lichen and moss that in time have covered the stone add even further to the sense of repulsion.

At the end of the path we find the large statue of Proserpine, goddess of Hell, who seems to be welcoming one with open arms as she stares into her kingdom.

The park was left completely abandoned for many years; it has recently been restored and is open to the public.

GARDEN OF THE VILLA CAPPONI (Florence)

The villa was formerly a typical 15th century building consisting of a house and tower. When Gino Ludovico Capponi bought it in 1572, he transformed and enlarged the building and created the spacious garden behind the house.

The owners that followed were responsible for modifications of the building constructing two loggias, one in front and one behind the villa. The transformations, in this particular case, improved the appearence not only of the villa but also the garden that has kept its style typical of a 16th century Italian garden. In fact, we still find the high wall that encloses it and the division of terraces that create three distinct and attractive areas.

The first terrace consists of a large lawn from which is enjoyed a beautiful view of Florence.

Alongside this terrace is the lemon garden with beds of box-hedges, characteristically enclosed by a high wall covered with rose and wistaria vines.

The third part is a small "secret garden"; enclosed by walls on all four sides are wistaria plants, hedges and the inevitable fountain.

Recently, other small gardens have been created on a lower level; equally rich in flowers and box-hedges, they maintain the unaltered harmony typical of the grounds.

The garden is privately owned.

DELLA GHERARDESCA GARDEN (Florence)

The origin of the garden dates back to 1472 when the land was purchased by Bartolomeo Scala, a politician in the court of Lorenzo the Magnifico. A beautiful country villa was built, surrounded by large flower and vegetable gardens with many rare plants adjacent to the city walls in the area of Porta a Pinti. Today Via di Borgo Pinti is one of the many side streets that lead into the wide avenues that encircle the historical center of Florence.

In the 18th century the building was enlarged; the following century witnessed a radical change of style when the garden was submitted to the demands of the fashionable Romantic style of that time. The Count Guido Alberto Della Gherardesca, whose family had acquired the property 200 years prior, transplanted exotic plants that enhanced the grounds even further, as well as building two small temples, a coffee house, a tepidarium, fountains and a small hill from which one can enjoy the landscape of the surrounding park.

When, in the 19th century, the architect Poggi leveled the old walls of the city in order to build wide avenues, the garden shared a border with the Piazza Donatello. With the walls gone, a large entranceway was opened from which one can still glimpse the beauty and rarity of the vegetation within (among which are cork, yew and sequoia trees).

Today the park is privately owned and is used as administration offices.

GARDEN OF THE VILLA GAMBERAIA (Settignano, Florence)

The villa was formerly a modest farmhouse belonging to the monks of Saint Martin of Mensola. In 1400 it was purchased by the Gamberelli family in whose possession it remained until 1600 before passing onto the family of Zanobi d'Andrea Lapi. In 1717, the new proprietors, the Capponi, restored and enlarged the villa, giving it its current Florentine appearance. It was during this period that the park, created by the Lapi family, was enlarged and embellished with statues, fountains, water games and a small grotto.

One can still follow a stately avenue lined with cypresses before reaching an observation point: a high hedge pruned into the shape of a tunnel has windows that overlook Florence and its surrounding countryside. The garden itself is not large, but it is a perfectly groomed jewel with skillfully pruned hedges. To one side of the villa is a secret garden and a small forest of ilex. The garden is private property.

GARDEN OF THE VILLA GARZONI (Collodi, Lucca)

The creation of this garden dates back to the middle of the 17th century and the desire of the Marquis Romano Garzoni. It was modified by the architect Ottavio Deodati in 1786.

It is a typical example of an Italian Baroque garden, particularly unusual for its grounds.

Its principle characteristic is represented by the wealth and sophistication of its vegetation, such as an avenue of palm trees and a small forest of bamboo. Also of interest are the plants artistically pruned into geometric and animal shapes, typical examples of topiary art.

Above on both sides we find hedges and flower beds in the design of the Garzoni coast of arms.

Further up, we can admire the three flights of elegant staircases constructed in a Renaissance style and harmonizing well with the garden. They are decorated with terracotta statues, shells, grottos and waterfalls.

It is all dominated by the large statue of Fame, from whose trumpet bursts a strong jet of water. Just below, Deodati built a flight of stairs using water effects; on either side are two large statues that represent the two rival cities of Florence and Lucca.

In the garden we find a labyrinth, a small suspended bridge and a small theatre carved out of the forest with statues from Greek comedy and tragedy. The garden is open for visits.

GARDEN OF THE VILLA LA PIETRA (Florence)

The villa dates back to the early 1400's. The first owners were the Sassetti and then the Capponi (1697), followed by the Incontri.

It was Sir Arthur Acton who, upon buying the property in the early 1900's, created the outstanding Italian garden with statues, hedges, stairways, loggias, arches and columns, ponds and open vistas of nearby Florence.

Previous alterations had transformed the open, green area into the "typical" English garden according to the demands of the time.

Fortunately, in 1907, the brave decision of the new English owner restored this incomparable artistic and naturalistic monument to its original style. It is conserved today with loving and competent attention by the son, Sir Harold Acton. As he likes to point out, the garden is predominantly composed of evergreens.

The garden's major attractions are, in the perfect style of the Italian garden, its precious statues.

The oldest garden is to the north. Inspired by Capponi, it is the perfect "hortus conclusus" or secret garden. Encircled by high walls, it is used today as both a vegetable garden and 'limonaia' or lemon tree greenhouse.

In a charming green theatre, statues who seem to be performing their roles in a comedy of fantasy, peek from the wings.

The villa's facade is typical of the 17th century Tuscan Baroque style although many details inside date back to the construction of the house almost two centuries before.

The garden may be visited upon arrangement with the owner.

MEDICI GARDEN OF BOBOLI (Florence)

It was only after the marriage of Cosimo I and Eleonora of Toledo in 1549 that the enlargement of the palace (initiated in 1457 by Luca Pitti) was resumed under the direction of Ammannati. Following Cosimo's wish, the land behind the palace was to be transformed into a garden and was entrusted to the famous architect Niccolò Pericoli, also called "Tribolo": his task was to create a true paradise. Tribolo designed the park as if dealing with a landscape whose hedges and trees substituted the buildings and where statues, fountains and grottos were aimed at embellishing and enhancing such architectural elements.

When he died in 1550, the park was not yet finished and was entrusted to Ammannati and then Buontalenti to then be finished in approximately 1600 by Alfonso Parigi.

The Boboli Garden has been defined as "An open air royal palace."

Many things are worthy of mentioning: for example the amphitheatre where games, parties and shows took place. One can wander along ramps and terraces, each of which is distinguished by a fountain or by the small avenues of box tree that lead to the top of the hill, the belvedere; the fountain of Neptune is the work of Stoldo Lorenzi.

On the right, we can admire the fountain best known as the "Islet". It was conceived by Parigi as an aquatic garden enclosed by a wall of ilex trees, with citrus plants and statues. In the center above a large basin is the statue that represents the Ocean; the figures around him represent the Nile, Euphrates and Ganges Rivers.

The grotto of Buontalenti is unusual for its illuminations: the light comes through a circular hole made in the top of the grotto. The first of three rooms is made up of limestone and stalactites, and the statues of Michelangelo's "Slaves"; in the second room, covered with shells, a group of De Rossi's statues represent Paris and Helen. In the third room, a fountain reveals Giambologna's statue of Venus who is surrounded by four satyrs.

The garden is now public property and may be visited.

MEDICI GARDEN AT CAREGGI (Florence)

This villa was purchased by the Medici in 1417 from the Lippi family.

In 1457, Cosimo the Elder restored it, making it larger and embellishing it under the direction of the architect Michelozzo.

Michelozzo erased the building's primitive, fortified appearance, transforming it into a far more refined villa surrounded by a double loggia.

The garden was built in the typical manner of those times, with potted lemon trees, small avenues, laurel and fruit trees. Many rare plants were also cultivated in the garden: the fashion of that time dictated that all cultured men should become involved in the study of nature and its multiple aspects.

Lorenzo, nephew of Cosimo, made the villa a cultural center where the most illustrious men in literature, art and philosophy could gather. Famous guests included, among others, Poliziano, Leon Battista Alberti, Donatello, Pico della Mirandola and Vasari. Such places were conducive to cultural encounters, for the garden offered one the inspiration for meditation and study. After Lorenzo's death in 1464, the villa was practically abandoned until 1779 when it was sold to the Orsi. Other proprietors over the years have disfigured the garden by partially transforming it into a Romantic park.

Today, the villa is used by the administration of Careggi Hospital.

MEDICI GARDEN AT CASTELLO

The villa of Castello was purchased by Lorenzo and Giovanni, sons of Pier Francesco dei Medici, nephew of Cosimo the Elder. It stayed in this family until 1477, enriched by many precious treasures. Unfortunately, many of these treasures (such as the frescos by Pontormo and Bronzino) disappeared during the sackings at the time of the expulsion of Piero dei Medici.

The greatest wealth of this villa, however, is found in its splendid garden created in 1540 by Tribolo for Cosimo I, Duke of Tuscany, as an ornament for the villa itself.

Upon Tribolo's death, the direction of the work was entrusted to Vasari and was later completed by Buontalenti in 1592.

Even Vasari described it as "the richest, the most magnificent, the most ornate garden in all of Europe."

The garden has today undergone many modifications and is far from the testimony painted by Utens at the end of the 16th century; grottos, fountains, statues, labyrinths, secret gardens and orchards linked together to form one of the most beautiful examples of the Italian garden.

The "water games" were planned by Pietro di San Casciano, famous hydraulic expert of the time; they used the water supply at Castellina as well as the nearby Villa della Petraia in order to accomplish the ostentation of imaginative and creative effects. Tribolo's plans foresaw the presence of some 50 statues symbolizing the mountains and rivers of Florence, the virtues and arts of the Medici.

The garden was divided into three levels: the part closest to the villa was the place for repose and contemplation. It offered statues by Ammannati and Giambologna and was enclosed by high walls. Originally the nucleus of the garden, today only the green beds, box-hedges and potted lemons remain.

Above one can still find the "limonaia" or lemon shelter, hot-houses and grotto where Giambologna sculpted, in many different materials, groups of animals with unique, multi-colored effects.

On the third level is a small forest of ilex and oak trees with a central pond dominated by Ammannati's statue symbolizing Winter.

Unfortunately, nothing remains of two small secret gardens that were found on either side of the building. One was used for the cultivation of medicinal herbs under the auspices of the statue of Aesculapius, god of Medicine.

The garden is currentrly owned by the State and may be visited.

MEDICI GARDEN AT PETRAIA (Florence)

Originally a castle belonging to the Brunelleschi family was found on this site. Its main tower still stands.

The surrounding land was once farm land rich with crops of wheat, olive trees and fodder. The Strozzi passed the property onto the Medici in 1532. Fernando dei Medici inherited it from his father Cosimo and began its transformation into a princely villa and a garden by commissioning the work of Buontalenti (1535).

From the original lay-out there remains an area "wild with ilex and cypresses" and part of the large garden that was designed by Tribolo.

Particularly noteworthy is the slope that leads up to the villa, divided into three levels by G. Parigi in 1631. On the highest level where the villa stands, large vases of potted citrus trees embellish the lawn while geometrically shaped beds surround a fountain with a statue representing Florence.

A lower level is reached by a stairway and opens onto a plant nursery and numerous ponds or basins while the third level offers a large garden with Italian styled hedges.

The garden of Petraia was especially famous for its multitude of "water games" whether for decorative purposes or for the irrigation of flowers which grew in abundance, including rare botanical species and experimental plants.

During the Reign of Italy, the villa was the favorite residence of King Vittorio Emanuele II (1864).

Today the property belongs to the State and may be visited.

MEDICI GARDEN OF POGGIO A CAIANO (Florence)

In former times, on the point where the villa now stands, there rose a castle belonging to the Cancellieri of Pistoia.

It was first sold to the Strozzi who transformed it into a country villa called "Ambra" and then to the Rucellai. It was only in the latter part of the 15th century that it became the property of Lorenzo the Magnifico who entrusted the various transformations to Giuliano da Sangallo. This project confirmed the ideas and talents of this gifted architect: the strength of the colannade that circles the building at its base points out the brilliance of the facade and the elegance of the small open gallery crowned by a frontispiece with a terracotta frieze of allegories.

With theatrical effect, the stairways introduce the building into the park stretched before it, creating a proper relationship with the natural surroundings.

The garden behind the villa was transformed in the 19th century into an English park, extending to the banks of the Ombrone.

On the right side of the villa is an Italian garden with large vases of lemon trees and a central basin or pond.

The villa was used as a hunting lodge or as a stop-over on the road between Florence and cities of the Tuscan coast. It is especially remembered for the romantic love story between Francesco dei Medici and Bianca Cappello.

During the Reign of Italy, the villa passed onto the crown; King Vittorio Emanuele II and the Countess Mirafiori were its most celebrated guests.

It was during this period that some restorations were done, somehow disfiguring the beautiful rooms of the villa and altering the garden.

The garden has been property of the State since 1919.

PRATOLINO PARK-VILLA DEMIDOFF (Florence)

The Prince Francesco dei Medici was himself actively involved in the transformation of the park during the first twenty years after its purchase in 1568. With the help of a team of exceptional artists such as Buontalenti and Giambologna and myriad devices, he changed a land that was once *"uncomfortable, sterile, hilly, barren and wanting in water"* (Montaigne) into a sort of enchanted garden of wonders.

An inedited and very heterogeneous representation of allegorical characters took shape: pagan gods, mythological heros (Jupiter, Pan, Perseus, Juno, Cupid) and a mixture of humble protagonists, both man and beast, representing rural life (the washerwoman, the farmer, the frog).

Little remains today of the park's wonders: the astonishing colossal Appenine, with his grottos and room inside his head; Jupiter's pool; Cupid's grotto; the fish pond of the Mask and the structures used as the Chapel, Pages' Quarters, the Inn, the Stables, etc. Late 16th century documents by Raffaello Gualterotti and Francesco de Vieri confirm that the Mannerist park was immediately the center of attention for botanists, scientists, artists and eccentric travellers, from Aldrovani to Montaigne, Schickhardt to the Marquis de Sade and Ludwig of Bavaria to Leo von Klenze.

The villa and its chattering grottos populated with fascinating automatons were almost immediately threatened by the same waters that once gave it life. After a long struggle it was demolished in 1824 by Ferdinando III dei Lorena, at the same time that a radical renovation program had been launched by the Bohemian gardener Giuseppe Fritsch.

The last of the Lorraines attempted a come-back in a neoclassical vein, building the elegant country home of Montili (by Luigi De Cambray Digny); destined to have replaced the detroyed Medici Palace, its original plans have been saved.

After Italy was united, the compound became the property of the Demidoff family who purchased it in 1872. They attempted to reconstruct the Pages' Quarters and the Royal Residence (this became the "Villa Demidoff" with a monumental solon designed by Enrico Ceramelli and Luigi Fusi), and attended to the restoration and maintenence of the garden.

Then after the last war, decadence: in 1955 the property passed from the Demidoff to the Karageorgevich and was abandoned and dismantled for the auction of its precious furnishings in 1969. A short-term ownership by the Società Generale Immobiliare failed and in 1981 the Province purchased the whole lot. They have been actively involved in the complex task of recovering the structures and the park which has been reopened to the public. Today, Pratolino is the site of concerts, conventions and exhibitions enthusiastically attended by the public; it is intended to be the new "laboratory of wonders".

GARDEN OF SANTINI TORRIGIANI (Camigliano, Lucca)

The villa belonged to the Buonvisi in the 16th century and was then passed onto the Santini. In 1816, Vittoria Santini married into the Torrigiani family who are the current owners today.

The villa, a rather squarish structure, has a facade whose picturesque statues are set into arched niches.

The area before the entrance was transformed into an English meadow; the avenue lined with cypresses still leads to the stately gates.

Alongside the building is the garden in its original French design, with basins, fountains, open spaces of flowers and beds of box-hedges.

The garden is private property but may be visited.

TORRIGIANI GARDEN (Florence)

The garden was born in the 18th century from the hand of the architect Fallani. It was illustrated in 1783 by Zocchi as a typical example of a Renaissance garden.

In 1817, Marquis Pietro Torrigiani commissioned de Cambray Digny to adapt the garden to the style of that time. It was widened, removing many of the bushes that lined the Via del Campuccio, then used the debris to build an artificial hill just next to the powerful walls of the city in the southern part of Florence.

And so was born an English park; the architect Baccani built a medieval tower on the graceful hillock.

Among its many splendors, the designer described a grotto that, "imitating Merlin's, the wizard of the poet Ariosto, entices the curious visitor to read a verse written on the rocks, subjecting them to a shower from various spurts and water tricks that are triggered by those adjacent".

The aim of the park's plan was to create an allegorical significance, with spaces that stimulated amusement, reflection and the rejuvenation of physical strength.

Today, one can still recognize the double nature of the garden in the beautiful rotunda with the allegorical statues of the seasons, an inheritence from the original Italian styled garden, facing the four directions of the compass. Equistrian shows were frequently held in the rotunda. The outer area adjacent to the walls is divided into small fields in a naturalistic English manner.

The garden is privately owned.

GARDEN AT THE VILLA REALE (Marlia, Lucca)

The villa originally belonged to the Buonvisi but was sold to the Orsetti in the 17th century. They were responsible for the large, Baroque garden whose highlights are a large pool with statues representing the Arno and Serchio Rivers, small waterfalls and fountains, a small theatre, lemon garden and stately statues and hedges.

A small but compact 'green theatre' was the site of many shows. One can still admire the statues of three characters of the Commedia dell'Arte: Pantalone, Pulcinella, Colombina.

The 17th century 'theatre of water' is majestic with its monumental fountains in the shape of a stone amphitheatre and imposing statues of Saturn, Jupiter, Adonis and Pomona.

In 1811 Elisa Bacicchi, sister of Napoleon Bonaparte, Princess of Lucca and Piombino and then Grand Duchess of Tuscany, purchased the villa and garden. She commissioned the architect Morel to 'remodernise' it, enlargening the space dedicated to the garden and subsequently expanding the waterworks and fountains.

The Renaissance gardens of the adjacent 'Bishop's Villa' (today used as an agricultural farm) were destroyed in order to substitute small woods and meadows that were typical of English parks.

Every kind of exotic plant imaginable arrived from all over the world. Many statues took their residence in the gardens, made of the fine white marble from the quaries of Carrara that experienced renewed recognition due to the Princess. Harmoniously united, the Italian and Romantic garden successfully coexist in this way.

The garden at the Imperial Villa was the site of grand receptions and numerous concerts (Niccolò Paganini, among many, performed here).

The compound then passed onto the Bourbons, the Dukes of Parma, the Lorraines and afterwards the House of Savoy (King of Italy).

Since then it has been called the 'Villa Reale' or Royal Villa.

The garden may be visited and admired for the care and competence given it by its present owners.

HORTI LEONINI (San Quirico d'Orcia, Siena)

This park-garden was built in 1540 by Diomede Leoni. Its surrounding wall at one point actually becomes part of the original walls of the town which, in that time, was governed by the Cardinal-Grand Duke Ferdinando I dei Medici.

The garden is designed in two levels: the lower of the two is divided into perfectly geometrical beds of box-tree, practically wedged into the triangular space made by the walls. The statue in the middle is of Cosimo III dei Medici. The higher level, built on a hillock next to the walls' look-out tower (today partially destroyed) is composed of a small wood of ilex or holm-oak. It is approached by a stately, central stairway; other stairs with wooden steps are still preserved in the medieval style when they were used to reach the highest points of the garden, enabling one to enjoy its beauty from above.

Today the garden is public property and open for visits.

BIBLIOGRAPHY

GENERAL TEXTS

A. CHIARUGI, *Le date di Fondazione dei primi orti botanici del mondo,* Pisa, 1543.

L. MABIL, *Teoria dell'arte dei giardini,* Basano, 1801.

G. ANGUILLESI, *Notizie storiche dei palazzi e delle ville appartenenti alla S.R. corona in Toscana,* Pisa, 1815.

M. DE BENEDETTI, *Palazzi e Ville Reali d'Italia,* Firenze, 1911.

E. PHILLIPS, *The Gardens of Italy,* A.T. Bolton, Country Life, London, (N.Y. 1919).

G. MASSON, *Giardini d'Italia,* Milano 1961 (Cenami a Saltocchio, Reale di Marlia, Torrigiani a Camigliano, Garzoni a Collodi).

F.H. HAZLEHURST, *Jacques Boyceau and the French Formal garden,* University of Georgia Press, Athens, 1966.

M. TOMMASEO, *L'arte dei giardini in bellezza e civiltà,* Firenze, 1857

G.C. ARGAN - M. FAGIOLO, *La strutturazione della natura. Schemi astratti,* in *Storia d'Italia* Einaudi, I, Torino 1972.

E. BATTISTI, *Natura artificiosa to Natura artificialis,* in: The Italian Garden (First Domberton oaks colloquium on the History of Landscape Architecture) Dumberton Oaks, 1972.

G.C. ARGAN, M. FAGIOLO, *Natura e città in Storia d'Italia,* vol. 1 Einaudi, Torino, 1972.

M. DETIENNE, *I giardini di Adone,* Einaudi, Torino, 1975.

C. CONFORTI, *Le residenze di campagna granducali,* in "Città, ville, e fortezze della Toscana nel XVIII secolo" Firenze, 1978.

W. KUYPER, *Dutch Classicist Architecture. A Survey of Dutch Architecture, Gardens and Anglo-Dutch Relations from 1625 to 1700,* University Press, Delft, 1980.

F.H. HAZLEHURST, *Gardens of Illusions: the Genius of André Le Notre,* Vanderbilt University, Nashville, USA, 1980.

E. DE JONG, *Virgilian Paradise: a Dutch Garden near Moscow in the Early 18 th Century,* in Journal of Garden History n. 4 (1981).

G. RAGIONIERI, *Il giardino storico italiano,* Olschki, 1981.

B. BASILE, *Il giardino come paesaggio,* in "Paesaggio: immagine e realtà", Milano, Electa 1981.

J.B. BURY, *Some early Literary references to italan gardens,* Journal of garden history vol. 2 n. 1 1982.

M. DUVAL, *The King's garden,* University press of Virginia, Charlottesville U.S.A. 1982.

M. FACCINI, *Guida ai giardini d'Italia: alla scoperta dei giardini storici e moderni, degli orti botanici e della oasi naturali,* Milano, Ottaviano 1983.

A.V.V., *Testimonianze benedettine in Toscana oggi,* supplemento Rivista Ulivo, Asciano, Siena, 1980.

BASIC REFERENCES

L. DAMI, *Il Giardino Italiano,* Milano, 1924.

M.T. CRUCIANI BORIOSI, *La realizzazione Cinquecentesca del giardino Italiano,* in Antichità Viva 1.1962. EDAM, Firenze.

M.T. CRUCIANI BORIOSI, *I giardini dell'Italia centro settentrionale di derivazione tosco romana,* In: Antichità Viva 9, 1970, EDAM, FIRENZE.

G. FANELLI, *Firenze architettura e città,* Vallecchi, Firenze, 1973.

G.C. LENSI ORLANDI, *Le Ville di Firenze,* Vallecchi, Firenze, 1978.

M. FAGIOLO, *Natura e Artificio,* Officina, Roma, 1979.

G. FANELLI, *Le città nella storia d'Italia: Firenze,* Laterza, Bari, 1980.

H. JOHNSON, *The Principles of Gardening,* Beazley, London, 1980.

M. MASTROROCCO, *Le Mutazioni di Proteo,* Sansoni, Firenze, 1981.

F. CHIOSTRI, *Historie des jardin,* Dernoel, Paris 1981.

F. CHIOSTRI, *Historie des jardin,* Dernoel, Paris 1981.

E. SERENI, *Storia del paesaggio agrario italiano,* Laterza, Bari, B.U.L. 1982.

B.M. NOBILE, *I giardini d'Italia,* Calderini, Bologna, 1984.

Il Giardino Storico Italiano, Atti del convegno di San Quirico d'Orcia (SI), Ott. 1978, a cura di G. Ragionieri, Olschki, Firenze, 1981.

MEDICI VILLAS

G. CAROCCI, *I dintorni di Firenze,* Firenze, 1906.

M. FORESI, *Ville Medicee: Drammi e avvenimenti principali che si svolgono in esse,* Firenze, Uffici della Rassegna Nazionale 1908 (Estr. Rass. Naz. Fasc. 16 gennaio 1907 e 16 dicembre 1908).

M. DE BENEDETTI, *Palazzi e ville reali d'Italia,* Firenze, 1911.

J. RUSCONI, *Le ville Medicee,* Libreria dello Stato, Roma, 1938.

A. FARA, *L'architettura delle ville buontalentiane nei documenti,* in Città, ville e fortezze nella Toscana del XVIII secolo, Firenze, 1978.

C. CONFORTI, *Le residenze di campagna dei Granduchi,* in Città, ville e fortezze nella Toscana del XVIII secolo, Firenze, 1978.

D. MIGNANI, *Le ville Medicee,* Arnaud, Firenze, 1980.

A. GODOLI, A. NATALI, *Luoghi della Toscana medicea,* Firenze, 1980.

A. CONTI, *I dintorni di Firenze, arte, storia, paesaggio,* Firenze, casa Husher, 1983.

BOBOLI GARDEN

G. CAMBIAGI, *Descrizione dell'imperiale giardino di Boboli,* Stampa Imperiale, Firenze, 1757.

F.M. SOLDINI, *Il reale giardino di Boboli nella sua pianta e nelle sue statue,* Multigrafica, Roma 1976 (Ristampa dell'Edizione – Firenze, 1789) VASCELLINI FI 1789.

F. INGHIRAMI, *Description de l'Imp. et R. Palais Pitti et du R. Jardin de Boboli,* Poligrafia Fiesolana, 1832.

Catalogo delle piante esistenti nell'I.R. giardino di Boboli, Firenze, 1841.

Catalogo delle Statue del R. giardino di Boboli, con la notizia dei loro autori, catalogo delle statue del R. Palazzo Pitti e della Galleria, Firenze, 1880.

B. BAROCCI, *Il Giardino di Boboli,* in "L'illustratore Fiorentino", 1912 - 1915.

N. TARCHIANI, *Palazzo Pitti e il giardino di Boboli,* in: "I Palazzi e le Ville che non sono più dei re", Milano, 1921.

Archivio di Stato di Firenze – Catalogo della Mostra documentaria e icono-grafica di Palazzo Pitti e giardino di Boboli, Firenze, 1960, a cura di F. Morandini.

D. HEIKAMP, *La Grotta Grande del Giardino di Boboli,* Antichità viva, Firenze, 1965.

F. GURRIERI, J. CHATFIELD, *Boboli gardens,* Edam, Firenze, 1972.

F. GURRIERI, *Il giardino di Boboli,* in Atti della Soc. Leonardo da Vinci, 1975.

D. HEIKAMP, *The grotta grande in the Boboli Garden, Florence; a drawing in the Cpp-per Hevitt Museum,* New York in the Commoisseur, 1978.

M. FORLANI CONTI, *Ancora sulla grotta grande di Boboli,* in: Prospetti-va, 16, 1979.

F. GURRIERI, *La grotta del Buontalenti nel giardino di Boboli,* Bertelli e Piccardi, Firenze, 1980.

C. CANEVA, *Il giardino di Boboli,* Becocci, Firenze, 1982.

VILLA LA PETRAIA

L. ZANGHIERI, *le "piante di Condotti" dei giardini di Castello e la Pe-traia* in Bollettino degli Ingegneri, 1971, n. 2.3.

F. CHIOSTRI, *La Petraia: Villa e giardino. 700 anni di Storia,* Olschki, Fi-renze, 1972.

C. TOSI, *Dintorni di Firenze. La villa la Petraia.*

CASTELLO GARDEN

C. FEI, *Villa di Castello,* Olschki, Firenze, 1968.

WRIGHT. D.R. EDWARD., *The iconography of the Medici garden at Ca-stello,* IH: Journal of the Society of Architectural Historians 34, 1975; S 314.

D. HEIKAMP, *La Villa di Castello,* in "l'Oeil" n. 151-153 (1967).

VILLA DEMIDOFF

G. NOEL, *Les collections du chateau de Pratolino,* in "l'Art Revue Illu-strèe". 1883.

G. BACCINI, *Pratolino, Capitolo d'anonimo,* Firenze, 1885.

C. DA. PRATO, *Firenze ai Demidoff,* Pratolino e S. Donato, Firenze, 1886.

G. IMBERT, *La villa medicea di Pratolino,* Firenze, 1908.

W. SMITH, *Pratolino* in "Journal of the Society of Architectural Historian-s" XX 1961.

M.G. DE LA COSTE MESSELIERE, *la Villa Demidoff,* in "l'Oeil" CLXXI, 1669, 41.

D. HEIKAMP, *Les Merveilles de Pratolino,* in: "Oeil", CLXXI, 1969, 16.

D. HEIKAMP, *Pratolino nei suoi giorni splendidi,* in: "Antichità Viva", 1969 n. 2.

D. HEIKAMP, *Leo von Klenze im Park von Pratolino,* in "Festschrift fur Margarete Kuhn", Berlin, 1975.

L. ZANGHERI, *Per una lettura iconologica di Pratolino,* in "Antichità vi-va", 1977.

L. ZANGHERI, *Pratolino il giardino delle meraviglie,* Gonnelli, Firenze, 1979.

COFFIN DAVID R., *The Wonders of Pratolino,* in "Journal of garden Hi-stor", 1981.

S. LENTINI, L. ZANGHERI, *Il Ritorno di Pan: ricerche e progetti per il futuro di Pratolino,* a cura di A. Vezzosi, Alinea, Firenze, 1985.

F. DE VIERI, *Delle meravigliose opere di Pratolino,* d'Amore, Firenze, 1586.

S. DE CAUS. *Les Raisons des Forces Movantes,* Paris, 1624.

B.S. SGRILLI, *Descrizione della Regia Villa,* Fontana e Fabbriche di Prato-lino, Firenze, 1742.

G. ZOCCHI, *Vedute delle ville e d'altri luoghi della Toscana,* Firenze, 1744.

LUCCHESE VILLAS

E. RIDOLFI, *Guida di Lucca,* Lucca, 1877.

I. BELLI BARSALI, *La villa lucchese dal XIV agli inizi del sec. XV,* in "Boll. del Centro di Studi per la Storia dell'Architettura", Roma, 1960 n. 6 pp. 14-36.

I BELLI BARSALI, *Guida di Lucca,* 2° ediz. Lucca 1970 (villa Guinigi e villa Buonvisi «al giardino»).

N. ANDREINI GALLI - F. GURRIERI, *Il giardino e il castello di Collodi,* Firenze, 1975.

La Villa lucchese e il suo territorio, Mostra organizzata dalla soprintendenza per i beni culturali e ambientali e dal Comune di Lucca, con il patrocinio del Dipartimento Istruzione e Cultura della Regione Toscana, Vallecchi, Fi-renze, 1977.

I. BELLI BARSALI, *Ville e committenti dello stato di Lucca,* M. Pacini Fazzi, Lucca, 1980.

I palazzi dei Mercanti nella libera Lucca del '500. Immagine di una città-stato al tempo dei Medici, a cura di Isa Belli Barsali, M. Pacini Fazzi, Luc-ca, 1980.

BOMARZO

F. COLONNA, *L'Historia di Casa Orsinì,* Venezia, M. Bevilacqua, 1565 (Padova 1964).

A. BRUSCHI, *L'abitato di Bomarzo e la Villa Orsini,* in "Quaderni del-l'Istituto di Storia dell'Architettura" nn. 7 e 9, Roma, 1955.

G. ZANDER, *Gli elementi...,* ibid.

F. FASOLO, *Analisi stilistica del Sacro Bosco,* ibid.

P. PORTOGHESI, *Nota sulla villa Orsini...* ibid.

M. CALVESI, *Il sacro Bosco di Bomarzo* in: "Scritti di Storia dell'Arte in onore di Lionello Venturi". Roma, 1956.

M. RIVOSECCHI, *Bomarzo...* in; "Capitolium", a XXX Roma, 1955.

L. BENEVOLO, *Saggio d'interpretazione storica del sacro Bosco,* in: "Qua-derni dell'Istituto di storia dell'architettura", 1955.

M. CALVESI, *Il sacro bosco di Bomarzo,* Roma, 1956.

A. BRUSCHI, *Nuovi dati documentari sulle opere orsiniane a Bomarzo,* in: "Quaderni dell'Istituto di Storia dell'Architettura", Serie X 55-60, Roma, 1963.

A. BRUSCHI, *Il problema storico di Bomarzo,* in: "Palladio" erano XIII fa-sc. I - IV 1963, pp. 85-114.

S. SETTIS, *Contribuio a Bomarzo,* in: "Bollettino d'arte" (serie VI, LI, I e II), 1966.

J. RECUPERO, *Il Sacro Bosco di Bomarzo,* Firenze, 1977.

I. PIZZETTI, *Il "Genius Loci" e la selva di Bomarzo",* in "Spazio e Socie-tà", sett. 1982.

N. MILLER, *The secret garden of Vicino Orsini,* in: "Daidalos" 3, 1982.

J.B. BURY, *The reputation of Bomarzo,* Journal of garden history, vol. 3 n. 2, 1983.

M. DARNALL - M.S. WEIL, *Il sacro Bosco di Bomarzo* Its 16 th -- Century Literary and antiquarian context, Journal of garden history vol. 4 n. 1, 1984.

MIDDLE AGES

F. CRISP, *Medieval gardens,* Hacker Art Books, New York, 1979.
T.MC. LEAN, Medieval Englisch Gardens, Collins, London, 1981.

HUMANISM AND THE RENAISSANCE

FRANCESCO COLONNA, *Hypnerotomachia Poliphili,* ediz. Venezia 1499.
V. ARNTZ, *Italienische Renaissance Garten,* in: "Die Gartenkunst", 1910, n. 2
A. LE BLOND, *The old Gardens of Italy how to visit them,* B.T. Batsford, Ldt., London 1912.
A. LE BLOND, *The Old Gardens of Italy in Florenz,* "Mittailungen des Kunsthistorischen Institutes in Florenze", 1912 - 1917.
A. FARA, *Le ville di Bernardo Buontamenti nel tardo Rinascimento toscano,* in: "Storia dell'Arte", Berlin, 1975.
I. BELLI BARSALI, *Baldassarre Peruzzi e le Ville Senesi del '500,* Archivio Italiano dell'arte dei giardini, San Quirico d'Orcia, 1977.
T. COMITO, *The idea of the garden in the Renaissance.* Rutgers University press 1978.
P.F. WATSON, *The Garden of Love in Tuscan Art of the Early Renaissance,* Art Alliance Press, Philadelphia, 1979.
D.R. COFFIN, *The "Lex Hortorum" and access to gardens of Latium during the renaissance,* "Journal of garden history", vol. 2 n. 3, 1982.

BAROQUE

W.H. HARRIS, *A Description of the King's Royal Palace and Gardens at Loo,* London, 1699.
M.T. CRUCIANI BORIOSI, *La realizzazione barocca del giardino italiano e la sua parziale discendenza dalla contemporanea scenografia,* Firenze, 1963.

ROMANTIC GARDEN

MASSON, *Florentine and Tuscan Gardens of the Seventeenth and eighteenth centuries,* in Apollo 100, 1974.
E. SILVA, *Dell'arte dei giardini inglesi,* Longanesi, Milano 1976.
L. FLEMING, A. GORE, *The English Garden,* M. Joseph, London, 1979.
W. M. ADAMS, *The French Garden 1500-1800,* Scolar Press, London, 1979.
N. TEMPLE, *John Nash and the Village Pictoresque,* Alan Suttor Publishing, Gloucester, 1979.
W. COBBETT, *The English Gardener,* Oxford University Press, London, 1980.
E. MALINS, P. ROWE, *Irish Gardens and Demesnes since 1820.* Barrie and Jenkins, London, 1980.
P. BUSSADORI - P. ROVERATO, *Il giardino romantico e Jappelli,* Antoniana S.p.A. Padova, 1983.

PHILOSOPHY OF THE GARDEN

F. PONA, *Il paradiso de' fiori, overo lo archetipo de' giardini,* Verona, 1622.
E. WRETZUCESCO QUARANTA, *Itinerario Spirituale di Polifilo,* in: "Atti dell'Accademia Nazionale dei Lincei".
Rendiconti CCCLXIV (1967) vol. XXII fasc. 7 pag. 269-83.
R. ASSUNTO, *Il paesaggio e l'estetica,* Giannini, Napoli, 1973.

B. LASSUS, *Jardins immaginaires,* Les presses de la Connaissance, Paris, 1977.
G. VENTURI, *Le scene dell'Eden,* Bovolenta, Ferrara, 1979.
F. FERRUCCI, *Il giardino simbolico,* modelli letterari e autobiografia delle opere, Bulzoni, Roma, 1980.
E. BAUMANN, *Lebende Gärten,* Verlag für Architektur, Zurich, 1980.
E.B. MOYNIHAN, *Paradise as a garden in Persia and Mughal India,* Scolar Press, London, 1980.
R. ASSUNTO, *Filosofia del giardino e filosofia nel giardino,* saggi di teoria e storia della estetica. Bulzoni, Roma, 1981.
J. PREST, *The garden of Eden: The botanic garden and the recreation of paradise,* Yale University press, New Haven and London 1981.
P. CAMPORESI, *Le officine dei sensi,* Garzanti, Milano, 1985.

LABYRINTHS

DE VRIES HILL, *Labirinti,* 1508.
Z. RINALDI, *Il labirinto,* Firenze, Ricci, 1935.
P. SANTARCANGELI, *Il libro dei labirinti,* Vallecchi, Firenze, 1967.

BOTANICAL

G. GATTESCHI, *Discorso sopra l'agricoltura,* 1552 M.S. Bibl. Naz. di Firenze.
G.B. TEALDI, *Discorso sopra l'agricoltura dedicato a Cosimo I de' Medici,* 1571. Bibl. Naz. di Firenze.
F. GARBATI, *Nasce presso lo studio Pisana nel XVI sec. la botanica moderna.* Pisa, Nistri, Cischi 1980.
L. TORGIONI, *Projects for botanical and other gardens: a 16th-century manual,* "Journal of garden history", vol. 3 n. 1, 1983.
C. LINNEO, *I fondamenti della Botanica,* Theoria, Roma. 1985 (Rist.).

SYNOPSES

C.C.L. HIRSCHFELD, *Das Landleben,* 1768.
C.C.L. HIRSCHFELD, *Theorie der Garten Kunst,* Leipzig, 1779.
L. VON SKELL, *Beiträge zur bildende Garten Kunst,* Munich, 1825.
Z. RINALDI, *Il giardino italiano-Sue origini, suo sviluppo e sue influenze negli altri stili,* Ricci, Firenze, 1938.
E. DE JONG, *Bibliography of Literature on Dutch, Landscape Gardening and Associated Topics between 1960 and 1981.* in "Journal of Garden History", I (1981), n. 4.

GARDEN LANDSCAPING

R. BERETTA, *Giardini,* Manuale di Costruzione e composizione, Comunità, Milano, 1959.
F. FARIELLO, *Architettura dei giardini,* Ateneo, Roma, 1967.
A. CHIUSOLI, *Progetti di Giardini,* 1ª serie, Milano, 1977.

MAGAZINES

Journal of Garden History - An international quarterly, J. D. HUNT, Taylor & Francis Ltd, London, 1981.
La natura dei giardini - Numero monografico di Rassegna, Electa, Milano, ottobre 1981.
Abitare il verde - allegato ad Abitare n. 232, Milano, marzo 1985.

GARDEN PROTECTION

Italia Nostra - *Atti del convegno Naz.; Tutela e valorizzazione delle ville e dei giardini italiani,* Tamburini, Milano, 1960.

M. R. BARKHOF, C.S. OLDENBURGER-EBBERS, *Plants for the Restoration of the Baroque Garden of the Palace of the Loo at Aplldoorn,* in "Journal of Garden History", I n. 4 (1981).

CONVENTIONS

M. BAFILE, *Storia e arte del giardino,* Atti del convegno nazionale di Storia dell'Architettura, Perugia, 1948.

The Italian Garden. - First Colloquium on the History of Landscape Architecture, Coffin, Waschington, 1972.

I paesaggi rurali europei, - Atti del convegno di Perugia (7-12 maggio 1973), Deputazione di Storia Patria per l'Umbria, perugia, 1975.

Park und Garten in 18.Jahrundart - Colloquim der Arbeitstelle 18.Jabrundert, Gesamthochschule Wuppertal. (Wurzburg, 1976), Winter, Heidelberg, 1978.

The feeling for Nature and the Landscape of Man, P. HALLBERG. Rudgvists Bokryckeri for the Royal Society of Arts and Sciences, Gothenburg, 1980.

EXHIBITIONS

Mostra del Giardino Italiano (a cura del Comune di Firenze), Firenze, 1931.

Alexander Pope's Villa. Views of Pome's Villa, Grotto and Garden: a Microcosm of English Landscape, marble Hill House, estate 1980 (Greater London Council, London, 1980).

QUOTATIONS

VERLAINE, *Poemes Saturniens,* Paris, 1866.

G. PASCOLI, *Canti di Castelvecchio,* 1903.

VIRGILIO, *Georgiche,* Milano, 1908.

COLUMELLA, *De Agricoltura,* Milano, 1910.

F.G. LORCA, *Libro de Poemas,* 1924.

OVIDIO, *Metamorfosi,* Firenze, 1927.

WASHINGTON IRVING, *Grandi scrittori stranieri,* UTET, Torino, 1931.

P.B. SHELLEY, *Poemetti e Liriche,* UTET, Torino, 1931.

M. MONTAIGNE, *Viaggio in Italia,* Bompiani, Milano, 1942.

S. QUASIMODO, *Ed è subito sera,* Mondadori, Milano, 1942.

G. BOCCACCIO, *Comedia delle Ninfe fiorentine,* Milano, 1964.

L. DE' MEDICI, *Scritti scelti,* Torino, 1965.

L. ARIOSTO, *Orlando Furioso,* Torino, 1966.

G. BARBERI SQUAROTTI, *La cornice del Decamerone e il mito di Robinson,* Torino, 1970.

A.A.V.V., *The Oxford Dictionary of Quotations,* Oxford University Prs, 3rd Edition, New York, Toronto, 1979.

D. PONCHIROLI, *Il libro di Marco Polo detto il Milione,* Torino, 1979.

U. ECO, *Il nome della Rosa,* Bompiani, Milano, 1980.

ICONOGRAPHICAL SOURCES

PIERRE DE CRESCENCI, *Opus Ruralium.*

Romanzo della rosa, commodorum, 1480.

F. COLONNA, *Hypnerotomachia Poliphili,* 1499.

L. DE SAXONIA, *Lever. Jhesu Cristi,* 1503.

Eremus Camatodensis Moutis; Coronae in agro Perusino, 1530.

Adamo ed Eva in Paradiso Holbeih, 1540.

THOMAS HILL, *Tudor Garden,* 1558.

Dydimus Mountaine, the Gardener's Labyrinth, London, 1586.

Sacra Camaldulensis Eremus 1602.

BENNETT WOODCROFT, *Pneumatica,* 1851.

ERIC GILL, *Hortus Conclusus,* 1925.

Abitare il Verde - allegato ad Abitare n. 232, Milano, marzo 1985.

L O C A T I O N S